It is my birthday

Bobbie Kalman

🌳 **Crabtree Publishing Company**

www.crabtreebooks.com

Created by Bobbie Kalman

Author and Editor-in-Chief
Bobbie Kalman

Educational consultants
Joan King
Elaine Hurst
Reagan Miller

Editors
Joan King
Reagan Miller
Kathy Middleton

Proofreader
Crystal Sikkens

Design
Bobbie Kalman
Katherine Berti

Photo research
Bobbie Kalman

Production coordinator
Katherine Berti

Prepress technician
Katherine Berti

Photographs
iStockphoto: p. 14–15
Other photographs by Shutterstock

Library and Archives Canada Cataloguing in Publication

Kalman, Bobbie, 1947-
    It is my birthday / Bobbie Kalman.

(My world)
ISBN 978-0-7787-9418-9 (bound).--ISBN 978-0-7787-9462-2 (pbk.)

    1. Birthday parties--Juvenile literature.
I. Title. II. Series: My world (St. Catharines, Ont.)

GV1472.7.B5K34 2010   j793.2'1   C2009-906054-X

Library of Congress Cataloging-in-Publication Data

Kalman, Bobbie.
 It is my birthday / Bobbie Kalman.
    p. cm. -- (My world)
 ISBN 978-0-7787-9462-2 (pbk. : alk. paper) -- ISBN 978-0-7787-9418-9
(reinforced library binding : alk. paper)
 1. Birthday parties--Juvenile literature. I. Title. II. Series.

 GV1472.7.B5K35 2010
 793.2--dc22

                                          2009040956

Crabtree Publishing Company

Printed in China/122009/CT20091009

www.crabtreebooks.com   1-800-387-7650

Published in Canada
Crabtree Publishing
616 Welland Ave.
St. Catharines, Ontario
L2M 5V6

Published in the United States
Crabtree Publishing
PMB 59051
350 Fifth Avenue, 59th Floor
New York, New York 10118

Published in the United Kingdom
Crabtree Publishing
Maritime House
Basin Road North, Hove
BN41 1WR

Published in Australia
Crabtree Publishing
386 Mt. Alexander Rd.
Ascot Vale (Melbourne)
VIC 3032

Words to know

balloon   birthday party

cake

balloon
animal

candle   clown   present

It is my birthday.

I am having a birthday party.

I have five candles on my cake.
I am blowing out the candles.

I am eating my birthday cake.

I am getting a birthday present.

I am opening a birthday present.

There is a clown at my party.

The clown is funny.
He is making balloon animals.

When is your birthday?

How old are you?

Activity

Ask your friends to help you say happy birthday. Use your body to make the letters and words.

You can also use your body
to make these words.
What do these words say?

Notes for adults

Birthday traditions
Among favorite days for many children are their birthday and the birthdays of their friends. Some have birthday parties with other children, and some celebrate with family. Ask the children what special birthday traditions their families follow, such as giving out "goody bags" or playing special games. Do they eat certain foods, dance, or dress in costumes? Do they have their parties at home or in other locations? Ask children to draw pictures of their birthday celebrations.

Mark it on a calendar
Ask children to name the months of the year. As each month is named, ask those whose birthdays are in that month to stand up. Which month had the most birthdays? With the help of the children, mark all the birthdays on a large calendar. Everyone can then see whose birthdays are coming each month and help them celebrate at school.

Gratitude dance
Ask children to think about what they have done since their last birthdays. This exercise will encourage them to reflect on their accomplishments and feel fortunate for all they have. Children could draw pictures of the best things that have happened to them since their last birthdays. The whole class could do a "gratitude dance" to show that they are thankful.